LIVING INSTEAD

POEMS
BY
WILLIAM
BRONK

NORTH POINT PRESS

San Francisco 1991

LIBRARY OF CONGRESS
CATALOGING-IN-PUBLICATION DATA

Bronk, William.
   Living instead : poems / by William Bronk.
      p.   cm.
   ISBN 0-86547-463-X
   I. Title.
PS3552.R65L58   1991
811'.54—dc20   90-49135

I am servant to the god; he does his own work.

CONTENTS

LIVING INSTEAD

ALL UNKNOWN

The Gods of the earth and the earth's Great Men
focus inchoate into fixed forms
we can see. I regard the forms but revere and am awed
by inchoate they come from—the form unseen.

FRAILTY

Mastery's our want—the common want.
Rather than be slaves to if only our own
weakness or weaknesses we find in the world,
to fears and frustrations, great gravities,
to ways and places unknown, all those
who seem to threaten us and to ugliness,
we want to master these, to know, be strong
and beautiful or find the one who is
and follow there, espouse that mastery,
cling and believe: the mastery is there
or will be soon.
                        Yet the frail world goes on
unmastered, unmastering, and so do we.
Better to love us both the way we are.

GREATNESS AND GLORY

Called great is the gift that makes prize boys
and beauty queens, gift thought to be
a Grace of God given to a special few
—oddly chosen though it sometimes seems—
but chosen, and the favor something theirs that they have.

And then we find that kind of favor pursued
ardently and avidly or a favor like
that favor with a little luck is also ours
in our own right if we work hard enough.

And we can wear it around and show those
others, we can bully the world or modestly
blush beneath the medals and honors we earned
for ourselves, accepting the glory with becoming grace,
mistaking ours for the glory of the world.
                                              And there is
a glory of the world.
                        And it isn't ours to have.

5

TRAVEL NOTE

It is winter now and this dinghy my
vacation spot in the middle of the sea.
Quiet waters much of the time and I
sleep a lot. No question but that
I do feel very much alone
even sometimes bored with the whole thing
but, time to time, I see big boats
go by and have no interest in them, as little
interest, I should think, as they in me.

EVEN SO

The god we need to learn to love gives
us no reason to—no knowledge, power, or other
magnificences: being female or male
or neither of these. If we come to love ourselves
we need to love ourselves in the same way.

FORMAL DECLARATION

No form we make is a form we can live in long.
We try to though: we call it real.

Other times, we say real is too rough, we make
a prettier place of our fantasies and defy
what was said to be real, needing a place to live.

The forms of art are not to live in
but only to hold how form is noble and is real.

THE CAMERA DOESN'T LIE

We are, of course, without any areness at all
and that's the only way we really are.

We pick at it though, not satisfied;
we need to try it out, to make sure,
breaking things apart, putting them back
together again, making differences,
an apartness, being other and against
the other we made, bettering it as a way
to better us. Or we put an against to be
as background the better to see ourselves against;

we point out ourselves in the photograph!

ONLYNESS

Once the ordinary and the everyday stop
making sense which they only ever did
only because we told each other they
were only common sense, well . . .

EXORCISED

Long ago, something in shadow behind
my open bedroom door used to make
as if to come out. It stays out now.
Comfortless, accustomed, we move around
each other. I as much as forget it's there.

THE IMPORTANCE OF NOT BEING

It is important that we die only to show its unimportance.

This is the silly point we make by dying and we can't deny its either premise.

Gods and heroes who intend its doing show it most clearly.

But even the simplest death declares it too.

UNFOUNDED

It is to live almost easy in a world
uncertain of what it is and not need to impose
an identity on it and have to defend in the need
a falsity not otherwise
worth the defense.
                    Circle the world, the self,
not finding or stopping, looking once more and again.

SURMISE

Horizontal doesn't matter; it
will drain out through my feet and I'll lie
there, empty bottle with no deposit to collect.

AFTER BACH

In the cello suites we learn the way despair,
deepest sadness, can and must be phrased
as praise, thanksgiving. Of course we knew
this anyway but mightn't have dared it on
our own.
          And the way the sadness can be in part
to accept the absence of One to say it to.

IDEOLOGY

Knowledge: an easy assumption offers itself
and we say yes. Other assumptions net
with this. We follow their lines and set up rules
of proof. We get maps and house-plans, charts
of organization, whole cosmologies.
We know where we stand!

We don't know anything.

COURTLY LOVE

The world is whom we love in our time there
and it may love us back or seem to.
But the world was loved before, knows lovers' style,
accepts extravagances, goes its way.

THE BOOK

book open
on the floor
pages loose
read some words
it's our book
one we're in
lot forgotten
wonder when
—where we are

THE BUYOUT

Remember how, at the time of the Civil War,
you could buy a substitute to serve for you?
Don't we do that anyway in the war
of the world where we make us a substitute in the roles
we play? The self might be picked on; they could wipe
him out, poor boy he is, ungroomed, unknown,
unknowing. Cover him up: attitude
and costume, certain knowledges assumed
proud him out and will go instead of him.

LIVING INSTEAD

Nothing much we can do about it so we live
the way old bones and fossils lived, the way
long-buried cities lived: we live instead
—just as if and even believing that here
and finally now, ours could be the real world.

THE LOOK BACK

When Orpheus and his Eurydice
walked up from the underworld, they thought
of the light up there, how beautiful it was,
how much they longed for, needed it;
but even so, they'd been a long time
in the dark, too long. They'd learned it needed them.

THE MISSING CREDENTIAL

We want to believe the real world has form
and we could discover it—fixed form.
Maybe that form would have different approaches to
it, the way we have tried in the past or, on its own,
take different guises but, underneath, we'd know
something solid and unchanging. What
can there be about form that makes us want that way?

CONTAINMENT

Even the numbers we add, subtract, divide
and multiply have to be taken on faith.
They haven't any proof outside themselves.

I tell my truth-seeking friend not to look
at anyone or anything except
his own mind. I question why I do,

Is it from thinking absurdities he'll find
—and contradictions—will let him give up proof,
be contained with marvels and rigors that there are?

WE ARE LOST WITH HIM

My lord is the ordinary, the green,
the dirt green grows in—it smells dirty—
and the trees that grow there, the wild flowers.

He is the everyday, the food and hunger,
all the weathers, the day light, the night dark.

We can change them. We go off
to make things and he is forgotten.

The things show our strength. He is easy to lose.

We are lost with him.

LIGHT-HEAVY

Half-past four
in the morning: crick, crick.
Must be the heavy step
of new light from the window
beginning to wash the floor.

IMPRESARIO

The world can never get enough of its
experiences; it's as though what
they are and how they come out were something unknown.
At any time it has the same scripts
playing again in a million versions. What for?
Because it thinks to learn, this time, a new
thing or because it just can't help
itself?
            It's hard on us. We act it out
and do the things it tells us to do—some
of them I'd just as soon not tell about.
And it's not about us; maybe if we did have
a life of our own we needn't go along with it
the way we do. We cry real tears
feeling the misery. We don't hold back: die.
Make it real. The good parts, too:
we throw ourselves in and we love it, we laugh
our heads off. It's nothing. Not, at least, for us.
Most of the time the world won't even pay.

HOUSE TOUR

Now come in here; see what you think. It's not
a room we use much. That was the way
with the old parlors. They *looked* unused though
and even unusable and this is not
that different from the rest of the house. But you see it's big.
And, all the stuff that's in it, it's always looked
half-furnished: no carpet, scatter rugs
and bare floor. And look at this: some kind
of clock they said when we came here. But it doesn't tick
and no numerals on the face. If this is the face.

PETITION

Let our hurt offer compassion for the hurt
we find in the world. The world is torn and the tears
are wider and deeper than any of ours. The world
is the whole world—nowhere to go for help.
And we are, too. I pray to the world for the world.

THE LIFE SURPASSED

Making a living is more than earning food
and a place to live. It's winning consent, begrudged
consent or ignored consent but still consent.
And making a living is making, is something made:
a place, a time, ways to be needed and used
in timely causes to hold the time and place
or make a better place more timely than that
because time passes and our time can be passed
in things to do as if to be alive.

MOONLIGHTING

Whoever writes the scripts plays games with them:

It's me all right, very intensely me
but I'm in some different stories from the daytime ones
and you're there too—I'd know you anywhere—
but it's often another town and you pretend
to be someone else I know or used to know.
The places assure us we know where we are and then
we take a turn and don't know where although
we've always lived there and,
                              waking up,
we know it was wrong. Or was it? We're not sure.

THE MAPLE TREE

Maple is the heavy tree, burly, big.
Even tall, they barely get off the ground.
I love their density, billowing
the way clouds look punchable,
their loud green in summer, bonfires in fall
and the way their roots come out and over the ground,
caress across that surface they hug.

OLD TESTAMENT

The gist of human finds any way to hurt
itself; pleasures aren't exempt, they lead
to miseries. The greatest cleverness
makes ways not tried before. No ecstasy
like horror—how it energizes us
and draws us together in work and righteousness!
For our own good we do the terrible things.

UNBELIEVER

We want to believe but the factual is a belief
less fact the farther in or out we push.
We fantasize a reality made out
to be simpler than that but it won't do
either and we haven't any reality.

PARTICULATE. INHUMANE.

Not in our humanity are we
related to all of whatever we seem not
to be—to strange people who live away
or closer, to trees and loathsome animals
and microscopic forms that combat us,
to even the huge, dense mass of rocks
and gases of the less than living perceived and not
perceived that make the universe: all these
and we are of a single substance not
substantial itself or even material.
Our stuff, all stuffs the same: energy,
in little charges, swarms in clouds of flies
around itself, unanalyzable
and not becomes but is whatever it is.

THE POWER AND THE GLORY

When we fight it isn't for money or principle,
for faith, for land, for love; we fight for power
—for its illusion: we don't have the power.
Just knowing we don't is reason enough to fight.
Give us a feel. We're willing to settle for feel.

FOR STEPHEN MITCHELL

The enlightened stumble and fall:
no flashlights in the dark,
blindly daytimes also.

LOVERS

This summer night has my warmth
and darkness, my waiting stillness, is not I
but other as I stand in it and as
it stands as well in me. When I go back
to bed I take it back to bed with me.

FOR DESPERATE PEOPLE

Oh God, who said not now when Martha and Mary
asked, have strength for others when you haven't come.

I AM

Sense in the world what was the world before
the creation of the world. Not the world but the world's
intention is the true world. We feel it here:
the uncreated still. The rest will go.

UNPERSONAL

The image is unimagined; that image is ours.
The name is nameless; we are the not to be known.
Man is woman. We are marvelous.

ADVICE

Anyway, keep walking not
because the way will get you to a place
that is a place but because there are things to see
that make the idea of place and having to get
to it seem silly. And people, too: they're not
the ones, of course, but well—wait till you see.

INCARNATE

We find things we didn't know we had.
We wouldn't know how to ask for fortuities
ungiven, unasked-for, just there.
Not even absence certifies Him.

CONCERN

We go to shape-ups mornings in case
the morning may have something for us. It does
usually. The jobs it puts us on
don't work out too well. You wonder why
it keeps on even so, how it can still
afford, after all these years, the loss
not just of property but life. Of course
we'll all die anyway but I've seen jobs
take lives as if they didn't matter, lives
too numerous to count. Nobody did.
And much as you quit or care you'd have to agree
to the claim it doesn't matter: the job goes on.

Yesterday morning I watched the morning light
mark with assertive light the bole of a tree.
Jobs and even lives were unconcern.

HABITATION

We are like houses to live in.
It lives in us; we are the house.
We thought we were tenants. That was all wrong.
We are living space: put up and torn down.
Something moves in, remodels us, moves out.
We can be crowded or holler with hollowness,
be numbered on streets or stand off alone.
We have facades, need paint, can be
designated landmarks with a nice sign.
There aren't any people; there are houses that house.

Tenant, I am haunted by your presences.

VISIONARY

Poems don't make by added post and beam
the whole barn or see the barn as built.
The most the poem can do is know within
itself, in certain joints, this fits with that.

THE WAY IT GOES

That the I should emerge from them has often been thought
the pressing concern, the most important event
in the history of the world. They don't always agree
with this: they contend who the I should be to emerge.
The I didn't mean to be selfish; it sacrificed
itself, knowing for sure what they needs.

PRECONDITIONED

If now you look for some heavenly
or otherwise afterworld you must
have believed too literally in here,
its times and spaces, shacks and palaces,
whatever it drove for, believed the things
that make a world were not devices, believed
they were somehow real and believed the world they made.

THE LIVES OF PLANETS

Mars, we learn, had water once
or so we think; no people though.
Here, on Earth, the polar caps can melt
and drown our shores. Planets don't need us
and we know it too. If we were to kill ourselves,
as well we may, tectonic plates that shake
us occasionally would grind for a long time.

EXPLORATION

The way Columbus or someone earlier
came to a place to be called a New World
though not more new than the old world was
—there all along and people living there—
is like the way a poem is come upon:
you think there's something there, you go see what.

SOJOURNER

He's hardly ever here but I have the house
and it's all I need. It does for me.
People think it's mine and I treat it so
—pay the taxes and all, keep it up—
it's not that much. Even if he never comes
other people do. And the house is here.

ON BEING NOT WORTHY

Nothing began with me nor will it end.

We are not person but clothes it puts on.

Loving each other flesh loves flesh unclothed.

In acts of worship god adores god.

MONITOR

I felt if I don't get out of bed it won't
happen and I didn't want it to. Not
that it was going to happen to me—I didn't feel
any personal peril—but I didn't want to watch,
to see it: something terrible. Well,
you get up and talk to people, look around.
Nothing much to happen. It goes away.

II

REFUGEES

The country we came to tolerates us if that's
the word. You might say ignores. They don't
either take us in or put us out. Of course,
the part they use is a long way off but you get
the feeling that someday they'll come and say that we
haven't any business here at all.
And they'd be right but here we are and you have
to live, live somewhere, and where're we going to go?

THE FOREST PRESERVE

Mainly, we float. Not lighter than air
in our grossness but lighter than water nearly. We drift
around in our mythical pools and cling sometimes
to other flotsam coming by, rafts of myth,
call them islands and pretend to be trees with deep
roots in the island ground. But we aren't trees.

IMMORTALS

Accuracy agrees that eachness
matters, thus affirms that no one
is unimportant. Accuracy says too
and at the same time, any or all
of us can go while something there goes on
not missing us as if we never were.
And it's true, in a sense we weren't. We never were.

HEARING HARDER

The words have shed some pieces from them now;
I puzzle what's needed back to make them sound.
And I'm still here just as I always was
but, as in the words, some wanted pieces are gone.

BEING UNBEING

As New York City, say, or anything else
we think of as big—the field of planets held
by the sun's gravity—is still too small
to make so much as a point in the ultimate chart
of physical big, so our body's count
of uncounted molecules of DNA
can't find a place, is nothing at all in all
of life and our only way to be is be
bodyless in a world that nowhere is.

BUT SOMETHING IS

To some extent, all of us take on its face
the everyday familiar actuality.
We don't question that, strange though it seems
sometimes. It's what we mean as the real world.

We don't get beyond it most days
or even feel there is a real beyond.

Then, a person there or an object of some kind,
a certain place, a new idea, may strike
with a greater force and we see the world again
differently in the light of that.
                                        What used
to be real isn't so real after all.
Nothing is and we know it. We don't know what
to do. Of course we go back to the old world.
What else? There isn't another place. Or a need.

REPERTORY COMPANY

To look at us now aren't we the colorless bunch?
Who would think we could play all the classical roles
we do—contemporary too—and switch
so easily from role to role? I guess
that's what it is for us: we act our part
when we get a part and, by God, you'd think it was real,
as though we were really being there on the stage
and making something happen, telling the world.

HYDRO-ELECTRIC

Often love is what we don't have
or what we lose. Maybe absence or loss
is where it is, is how we know love.
Sometimes its real power has to be
behind a great wall, stopped and held
back of a dam and powerless without.
The weight of the water conjures a thought of a flood:
things washed away in front of it.

LIARS

Variation is definition enough
for God and also for Man. The orthodox
try to narrow them down. They both slip out.

JOURNEY

It does add up but since we're traveling
anyway it's hard to realize
how again and again it's taken another year,
life, century—whatever—to have
us back in the oldest texts we know,
to read them again, register, be there.

GOOD FRIEND

In a room full of loud boasts he tells
me again some quiet jokes we used to hear.

LIFETIME

I have been reading about a poor boy
who lived a story of his life: rectitude,
solid achievement, very hard work.
Neighbors were proud of him. They watched it come
about as it did. It gave them something to believe.
They saw this as a true story and it was.
It was a story that he acted all out.

COVER-UP

We are moved close together in an underground
village where address is built of little more
than its specification forcefully listing us there.

PLAYBOYS

Before we go to sleep we want to be told
again some story we can find
us in. Don't leave us out. Conflict, yes,
and later triumph. Vicarious is good
as long as we see us there: we like to play.
Tomorrow we'll go to work making believe.

PROXIMITY

Listen, all of us have done some harms
to one another and done some goods and we've
intended them and seen them multiply
out-of-hand along the way, seen
them reverse themselves too: the harm to good
and good to harm or both together—mixed.
No need to look away for this: all human scale,
our work, what we might call in-house.

But there are times in the world when harm and good,
not focused on us, nevertheless intrude
much as if their hugeness happening
somewhere else were not contained there,
couldn't be, and a glance is seen of some
more central place we only lie near to.

MEATS

We, as living, visit us: we come
alive. We are the same who go away.
Meat we put on the table tells us this.

AT LARGE

We try to imagine this unimaginable,
this world. Some of us think we manage to
or, at least, come close. We do come up
with brave and glorious thoughts, with intricacies
of marvel and even gruff plainnesses,
great othernesses to tempt us to live instead
with orders and understandings offered to us.

And our lives here! Who could believe our lives!

DE SENECTUTE

Stuck overhead, a sky chart glows
in the dark. In bed, I gaze at the galaxy.

My bathroom floor was flooded and rained
through the kitchen ceiling beneath. I swept

the water away. Younger, I used to be puzzled
by the uncaring shabbiness of age.

HISTORIES

Time is what will take us but time is too
transparent to fight against: there's nothing there.
And we are spectral too. We make a stand,
materialize some troops and armaments,
assume an enemy and fight with him.
We want to be monuments affirmed in stone.

BEETHOVEN: THE LATE SONATAS

You have to understand it isn't what
he says but what was being said to him.
He even hardly had to write it down.
He listened in his deafness. In ours, we hear
him listening. We overhear.
The purpose for the pianist playing now
is how to let us think he isn't playing,
to just be quiet and listen along with us.

ASSEMBLY

Remembering people now including ones
dead a long time and ones told
to me I never knew myself, ones
I read or read about as well as those,
of course, I meet on the streets still, is good
to do.
        It's teacher checking the roll, it's
reporting the Company all present or
accounted for, it's filling the bus:
OK, all here, we can proceed.

WALKING. WAKING.

The way I want sleep is the way I'll want not
waking. But, for now, waking is still good.
In sleep's woods, waking's the open lake
of surprise. We intended only the woods' close.

COMEABOUT

The poems push their insistence now. I used
to despair in their long absences.
Now, it's go away! Let me alone!

INSYNTHETIC

We shift as the twelve moons do on the twelve
months, our phases uneven with the months' days.

In the seasonal samenesses nothing is same;
on the rigid calendar we move alive

as vines shape over the trellis shape.
We are nowhere here nor there in a space between.

WALLETED

We, as we say, familiarize ourselves
with ourselves. We have some pictures taken to keep.
Identify. Driver's license. Loves
and kids. Found on the body. Entry badge.

Books and movies, daily TV news,
any mirror has us. We find us there.
And all our studies, tribal, trivial,
even the most abstract, can make a face.

We are discontent not to say who we are.

DOMICILIARY

It's a short stay and not as though we're here
forever but reason enough for some concern
where we put down and where they put us up
—not only us but the rest of the party too.
But I've never been much of a one to complain and besides
it isn't *our* place. Some people act
as though this is where we ought to have it all
out. Right here. I'm more concerned
what goes on back there while we're away.
I guess I couldn't help that either though.

THE WANTED EXACTITUDE

The way we shade in and out of sleep
of course—that consciousness that without
much sense of shift takes one form
and others some of which we neither see
nor feel—and even more our shading first
to life then out—marks us as metaphor
and metaphor our medium where the world's
matter is forces not material
and measured time and space will lose themselves
in extensions not measurable. And so can we
be lost and the world lost without a loss.

Yet let our metaphor be accurate.

AUTONOMOUS

Truth doesn't say what it is; it lets us say
and doesn't even care if we're wrong. We can make
our own discovery and blame it on the truth
or keep on talking never finding out.
What we do doesn't change us anyway.

WISTFUL

In the drugstore rack is a postcard even of here.
I buy and send me one in my mind. This
is a postcard world. Everywhere. They come
in the mail. We study them. Not where we live.
Photos. Actual places. They wish for us there.

NO ONE WE KNOW

He that is nowhere is anywhere.
I do not find him everywhere he is.
In any place or person he is never alone;
he is their presence that has none.
I do not want him who is my desire.

PUTDOWN

Boundaries and checkpoints. What's
outside? Well, parts of us not
inside. That's why border-guards.
If we're going to have a space of our own
here and have it now we need to define
just what we are: be somebody. Those
pieces left out may well be ours
but let them in and what'll we get? Do you want
to vague off into the infinite?

MEMOIR

It seems to us our human sadnesses
should matter. And our exultations also?
Neither seems to, even to us
after a short time; we get over.

And, in their throwing away, old memories
plead a lost importance as if it was.
We try to believe them or make as if we do.
Unless we don't care and admit we don't.

FINDERS

There are stars at night. Way off. Again and again
they astonish us as if we hadn't known
they were there. This was the way, days, on the ground,
Henry found flowers. We find them, too, of course,
with the same pleasure. Stars are at night. Way off.

SIDE SHOW

They do use us—crowd scenes, that
kind of things sometimes—in whatever it is
they do. Or I guess they do. Who knows? They don't
tell us. The worse part though is things
we do apart from them: you work it up
and start to act it out—good guys,
bad guys. It changes. Nothing means
what you thought it means. They must be the ones
to make that kind of change. You feel a fool.

STORY DREAMS. NO TELLING.

The last few minutes of sleep are gone soon
but we may have a story to see and hear before
we get up from bed. The narrative of dream
will be almost anything. The important part
—what we want—is the feel of story and the being there.
When we're out and awake the story doesn't come
naturally to us. It's second hand:
we see a movie, read a book or if
we make a story up we make believe.

It's true there's a story feel in acts of love.

And, even more, times wide awake,
and nothing involving us, we become aware
of that not narrative nor needing one.

GULLIVER FOUND

This is Lilliput; some Gulliver
shows us how small we are. It says to us
how there is a big world all around
that we can sense our being in and sense
its little regard for us and what we do.

We don't affect that world, don't even know
what it does or whether anything.
We go about our own, unhindered
unless our failures and empty successes be
its work. Nothing of ours changes it.

That world around us isn't about us.

LIGHT

Things of the present reflect the presence's light.
When the present is past and dark the light is still.

SELFNESS

Think about ourselves on Earth Day
—how we are more expendable than trees,
as easily dirtied as water is or air—
an animal that other animals
don't care about, can't anyway.
Should we love us or let us go with earth?

MASTERS

These people say we have a deed
which was given to us long ago
—right at the beginning even—and because
of our importance the whole place is ours.

We gave the names to all the animals.

They also say that a later covenant
to the deed was made in order to insure us against
disasters that nevertheless happen still.

They have made careful inquiries about that.

Meanwhile, they feel that elsewhere in this huge
universe there must be other ones
of our importance that we should talk to
and that they may be looking for us as eagerly
as we have started looking now for them.

HOMECOMING

Eden too, even Eden, we
made up. It means we always wanted a place
and never have one—had to make them up
and stories about them: Troy, Jerusalem,
old world, new world, once found, believed, then lost.

PLAYTIME

In a presence vast beyond size, a presence that seems
an absence, we hide and play with us as dolls.
We give us names and addresses, dress
us up in clothes, make loves and resumes,
battles, furtively say where we came from
and tell each other stories about ourselves.

BOILED DOWN

It's not
about us.

It's what
we're about.

LUX PERPETUA

Shines.

DEBRIEFING

What happens is that just as you come into time
and space, you get a body of your own, your place
there so to say and bodies, little at first,
fuss a lot. Helpless then, they need.
Later, though less helpless, they still need.
In time, you get accustomed to the needs
but the other thing with bodies—maybe the same
thing from another aspect of the needs is all
the pleasures. Needs and pleasures take a big
space there. Strange, too, to me,
were growth and change. A few people object
to them but to most everyone else they seem
the natural thing, fulfilling, required.
Quite a trip. Good though, to get back.

Design by David Bullen
Typeset in Mergenthaler Imprint
with Meridien display
by Wilsted & Taylor
Printed by Maple-Vail
on acid-free paper